Table of Contents:

TFBC History ………………………………………………………………… 5

TFBC Archive (1996 – 2004) ……………………………………………….. 15

You Know You're a Band Nerd When ……………………………………… 63

Grayhair (a comic exclusive to *TFBC: The Arrival!*) ………………………….. 85

Credits ……………………………………………………………………… 101

TALES FROM BAND CAMP

THE ARRIVAL

BY AMY M. BROWN

TFBC HISTORY

Welcome to the first *Tales From Band Camp* publication!

I first started cartooning when I was seven, and around that same time I fell in love with marching bands. In 1980, my family moved to Athens, GA, and I went to my first Georgia Bulldogs game. One of my first memories of the games was watching the 300 plus members of the UGA Redcoat Band march into the stadium. I was hooked! I told my mother that one day I would be in that band, marching into a 85,000 plus stadium just like those members did in 1980. From then on, I probably spent as much time watching and listening to the band as I did the football game (and I really love the game of football, so that says something!).

My older brother was on the high school football team, so my parents took me to all of his games. I didn't mind, because not only did I watch the game, but I could watch the band too. I couldn't wait to get to wear that band uniform and be a part of the football experience! I started playing flute in the 6th grade band and switched to bassoon in the 8th. In high school, I picked up the mellophone my junior year for marching and then became drum major my senior year. I accomplished my dream of making the Redcoats and started UGA in the fall of 1991. Marching onto Sanford Stadium for the first time decked out in the Redcoats' uniform playing "Glory, Glory" was just as exciting as I thought it would be back in 1980 as a little girl sitting in the stands.

In high school I began to get a little more serious regarding my comics. Most of them were about my high school friends and teachers. I also did a band comic for each year of high school, which was basically a collection of inside jokes from that year.

Portion of yearly band comic from fall of my freshman year (1987):

I became officially published in college with the comic strip *Buster Bulldog*, which appeared in *The Red & Black*, the school newspaper. During that time, I also drew up band related comics, but I knew they wouldn't be approved because, honestly, only "band people" would get them. As I did in high school, I put out a yearly comic for the Redcoats. These comics were printed onto t-shirts and billed as the "Unofficial Redcoat Band shirt." You can see these comics on pages 11 and 12. The following comics are samples of my pre-TFBC work that is band related.

Mellophone t-shirt design that was never used.

Mellophone design from my junior year in Redcoats (1993):

Excerpts from 1991 Redcoat Band comic:

Excerpt from 1992 Redcoat Band Comic:

Excerpt from 1993 Redcoat Band Comic:

Excerpt from 1994 Redcoat Band Comic:

The comic *Tales From Band Camp* was officially born in 1993. I put together a small booklet of Buster Bulldog band comics and passed them out to Redcoat band members at one of the practices. I made a grand total of two issues! Some of the jokes in those issues made their way into early TFBC comics. TFBC first appeared on the World Wide Web in April of 1996. I was just starting off in "the real world" after graduating from the University of Georgia in 1995. Even though I didn't major in computing, I soon became a computer geek and wanted to know everything I could about the internet, which was just starting to enter the public's eye around that time. Mostly I was excited about the potential of "publishing" my band comics to the general public without going through traditional ways.

Originally TFBC started off featuring a college band. The original comic follows on the next page. As you can see, there are some elements like the graduate assistant, the secretary, and the "beer" comment (sorry parents!) that would be obviously part of a college environment rather than a high school one. Eventually TFBC morphed into a high school band, and the characters slowly gained names and personalities over time. I still like to think of TFBC as a work in progress.

Original title from 1996 (as you can see, the assistant director's name was different):

First TFBC web comic from April of 1996:

And now, the comics!

TFBC ARCHIVE

WHEN BAND ALUMNI COME
TO VISIT

Title art poking fun at my laziness.

You Know You're a Band Nerd When...

You automatically march to the background music at the mall.

You successfully name the interval of a car horn.

HEY, THAT'S AN AUGMENTED FOURTH!

BEEP!

At the movies you listen to the soundtrack rather than watch the movie.

MAN, LISTEN TO THOSE FRENCH HORNS!

You get excited about a marching band finale.

WOW, WHAT A FINALE!

YEAH!

Halftime is the most important part of a football game.

FOOTBALL TEAM? WHAT FOOTBALL TEAM?

You gossip about band directors.

DID YOU HEAR ABOUT MR. SHARPENFLATTE?

NO, TELL ME!

©ANDORE99

DAY ONE OF BAND CAMP

HOORAY! BAND CAMP IS STARTING! I LOVE BAND CAMP!

DAY FOUR

THIS IS FUN, BUT I DON'T REMEMBER IT BEING THIS HOT.

DAY EIGHT

SHUT UP! I *AM* IN LINE! YOU'RE NOT!

DAY TWELVE

AAAAAARRRGH! I *HATE* BAND CAMP!

©AMOORE99

WHY DO THE BELLS ON FRENCH HORNS POINT BACKWARDS?

SPLAT! SPLAT!

NEVERMIND.

©AMOORE99

IT HAS BEEN REQUESTED THAT FOR THIS MARCHING SEASON, WE PLAY SOMETHING OTHER THAN THE TYPICAL SPANISH OR PATRIOTIC SHOWS.

SO WHAT ARE SOME OF YOUR SUGGESTIONS?

BARE NAKED LADIES! LET'S DO SMASH-MOUTH! FAT BOY SLIM! KORN! MUSIC FROM *THE MATRIX!* RICKY MARTIN!

UMMM.. HOW ABOUT "AN AMERICAN SALUTE" OR "MALAGUENA?"

©AMOORE99

BAND DIRECTOR QUOTES

THE GOOD | **THE BAND** | **THE UGLY**

WITH APOLOGIES TO TOM BATIUK.

33

THE RAINCOAT INCIDENT

A *TALES FROM BAND CAMP* SAGA:

BEHIND THE MUSIC

I WOULD LIKE TO THANK ALL OF YOU FOR SHOWING UP THIS SATURDAY FOR OUR RECORDING SESSION.

BUT BECAUSE OF THIS SACRIFICE, YOU'LL HAVE A CD YOU'LL TREASURE ALWAYS – AFTER PURCHASING IT, OF COURSE.

I KNOW THAT YOUR TIME IS VALUABLE SO WE APPRECIATE THE TIME SPENT...

I HAD TO CANCEL MY SURGERY... OR ELSE.... *COUGH..*

@AMOOREBROWN

AND NOW, I'LL TURN THE PODIUM OVER TO MR. CULDESAC.

THANK YOU!

SO LET'S BEGIN! DAPHNE, COULD YOU GIVE US AN "F"?

SURE!

TWO MINUTES LATER...

I'M SORRY DAPHNE, COULD YOU GIVE US THAT NOTE AGAIN?

HEH HEH.. I LOVE DOING THAT.

GASP.. UH, OK.

@AMOOREBROWN

BEFORE WE BEGIN, I'D LIKE TO REMIND EVERYONE TO TRY TO CUT OUT AS MUCH EXTRANEOUS NOISE AS POSSIBLE.

READY? LET'S BEGIN WITH "LA BOUTIQUE FANTASTIQUE!"

=POP=
AH-CHOO! Shuffle
=THUNK=
=THUD=
~scrape~
Sniffle

MY KINGDOM FOR A BAND WITHOUT EXTRANEOUS NOISES.

HACK
=cough
TINK.

@AMOOREBROWN

36

Extra drawings from website pages

HOLIDAY CONCERTS

To the left is a page from my "scribble" book, or what I use when I think of ideas and need to remember them for later. I normally don't lay out the whole comic here - just something to refresh my memory.

As you can see, this is one that I used for the following comic.

@ABROWN

@ABROWN

43

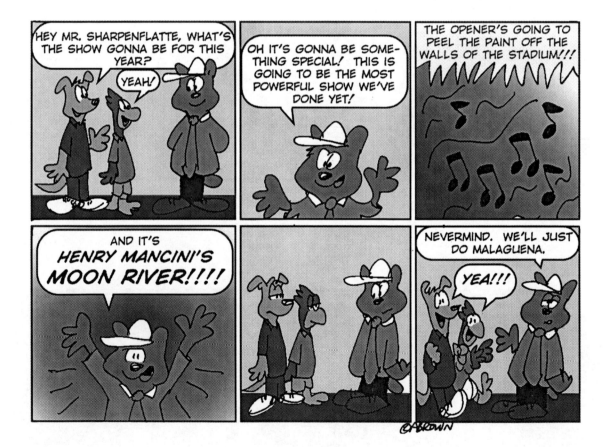

TFBC's Guide to Freshmen

"CLUELESS"

"THE WHINER"

"THE HYPER GUY"

"KNOW-IT-ALL"

Ideas from the scribble book that were nixed.

Drum Major Perks

GETTING TO WEAR A WHISTLE

HAVING A DIFFERENT UNIFORM THAN EVERYONE ELSE

ADULATION FROM THE FRESHMAN CLASS

SPENDING MORE TIME WITH THE BAND DIRECTOR

BAND CAMP
SUPPLIES:

PLENTY OF
SPORTS
DRINKS...

SUNSCREEN AND
BUG SPRAY...

SHH
OFF!

SUNGLASSES...

...AND ABOUT THIRTY T-SHIRTS
TO CHANGE IN BETWEEN
MORNING, AFTERNOON, AND
EVENING PRACTICES!

@ABROWN

I'D LIKE TO WELCOME EVERY-
BODY BACK FOR ANOTHER
YEAR OF BAND!

I HOPE EVERYBODY HAD A
GREAT SUMMER AND
PRACTICED HARD!

BUT BY THE LOOKS OF THE INCHES OF
DUST ON YOUR INSTRUMENT CASES, I
DOUBT THAT TO BE THE CASE...

@ABROWN

HEY, HAVE YOU SEEN THE NEW PIT
MEMBER?

NO, IS SHE ANY GOOD?

I'D SAY SHE WAS A NATURAL!

@ABROWN

56

Bus Trips!

TIPS FOR ENTERING...
THE UNIFORM ROOM

#1: BRING BRIBES AND CASH.

HEY, HERE'S A PRESENT... UMM, BY THE WAY... CAN I HAVE A BIGGER JACKET?

#2: IT'S OK TO LIE.

WELL, THE UNIFORM YOU RECEIVED WAS BASED ON MEASUREMENTS *YOU* GAVE US!

WASN'T ME!

#3: WATCH FOR TRICK QUESTIONS.

CAN YOU BREATHE? GOOD. NOW LEAVE.

GASP!!!!

#4: DON'T MAKE JOKES.

DO YOU HAVE IT IN ANY OTHER COLOR BESIDES RED? HAH HAH!

©ANOORE BROWN

REMINDER: THESE PEOPLE HAVE BEEN BREATHING THE SAME AIR FOR DAYS, SO TREAD CAREFULLY!

61

"YOU KNOW YOU'RE A BAND NERD WHEN..."

YOU DEDICATE A WHOLE SECTION OF A BOOK TO "BAND NERD" COMICS!

(WITH APOLOGIES TO JEFF FOXWORTHY!)

YOU SPEND SO MUCH TIME
IN THE BAND ROOM THAT YOU SET
UP A SMALL BED.

YOU HAVE THE BAND PHONE
NUMBER IN YOUR ADDRESS BOOK.

INSTEAD OF COUNTING SHEEP,
YOU THINK OF IDEAS FOR
NEXT YEAR'S HALFTIME SHOW!

THE LETTERS "H" THROUGH
"Z" DON'T MEAN ANYTHING
TO YOU!

YOUR IDEA OF A SATURDAY NIGHT
DINNER IS THE COLD HOT DOGS
AND WARM DRINKS SOLD AT
BAND COMPETITIONS.

YOU ROLL STEP DOWN THE
HALL IN TIME WITH OTHER
BAND NERDS!

ONE OF YOUR FAVORITE
PASTTIMES IS TO SING THE
SHOW WITH YOUR FRIENDS!

YOU'VE DOWNLOADED SONGS
YOU'VE PLAYED IN CLASS!

YOU KNOW AT LEAST 20
DIFFERENT WAYS TO FALL
ASLEEP ON A CROWDED BUS!

WHEN YOU HAVE BAND FRUIT UP THE WAZOO!

SIX OUT OF SEVEN CLASSES ARE IN THE BAND ROOM!

YOU TAKE YOUR INSTRUMENT
WITH YOU EVERYWHERE
"JUST IN CASE!"

YOU HAVE A VARSITY JACKET
FILLED WITH LETTERS, PATCHES,
AND BARS YOU'VE EARNED FROM
BAND!

YOU TAKE BETTER CARE OF
YOUR INSTRUMENT THAN YOU
DO YOUR CAR!

WHEN YOU ONLY CARE ABOUT
GRADUATION BECAUSE IT
AFFECTS YOUR CHAIR PLACEMENT!

YOU CAN NAME AND PLAY EVERY
SHOW YOU'VE EVER MARCHED,
BUT CAN'T REMEMBER YOUR HISTORY
LESSON FROM THE DAY BEFORE.

YOU KNOW THE PITCH OF
THE SCHOOL BELL!

YOU HEAR "THIS ONE TIME, AT BAND CAMP" A HUNDRED TIMES A DAY!

YOU PLAY ALONG WITH THE CD'S
YOUR BAND HAS RECORDED!

PEOPLE ASK WHO YOUR FAVORITE
BAND IS, AND YOU NAME YOUR
MARCHING BAND!

YOUR DEFINITION OF SKIPPING CLASS IS HANGING OUT IN THE BAND ROOM!

YOU DIRECT ANY SONG ON THE RADIO!

YOU HAVE A NECK STRAP TAN LINE!

ONE, WE ARE THE JAGUARS..
TWO... A LITTLE BIT LOUDER, THREE!

OABROWN

YOU'VE SAT THROUGH SO MANY FOOTBALL GAMES THAT YOU KNOW THE CHEERLEADERS' ROUTINES!

THE SMELL OF BUS FUMES BRINGS
BACK FOND MEMORIES
OF BAND!

YOU'VE CALLED YOUR BAND
DIRECTOR "MOM" OR "DAD" AT
LEAST ONCE!

YOU WEAR YOUR BAND SHIRT EVERYWHERE!

YOU MAKE BAND PHILOSOPHIES...

*"Field shows are like your youth;
you cannot fully appreciate their beauty
until you look at them from afar."*

WHEN PEOPLE WORRY IF THEY SEE YOU WITHOUT YOUR INSTRUMENT!

YOU HAVE NIGHTMARES ABOUT DR. BEAT!

IF REHEARSAL ENDS AT 9PM,
AND YOU DON'T LEAVE UNTIL 10PM!

WHEN YOU START DRESSING
LIKE THE BAND DIRECTOR!

YOU FINGER THE NOTES TO
YOUR PARTS IN MATH CLASS
(WITHOUT YOUR INSTRUMENT)!

YOU KNOW EVERYBODY IN BAND
ONLY BY WHAT INSTRUMENT
THEY PLAY.

YOU WAKE UP SUNDAY MORNING IN YOUR BAND UNIFORM!

WHEN YOUR DIRECTOR CALLS YOU A BAND NERD!

YOU RUN A WEBSITE THAT IS
DEDICATED TO BAND!

Exclusive to *TFBC: The Arrival*:

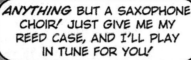

95

97

WRITTEN & DRAWN BY AMY BROWN
COPYRIGHT 2004

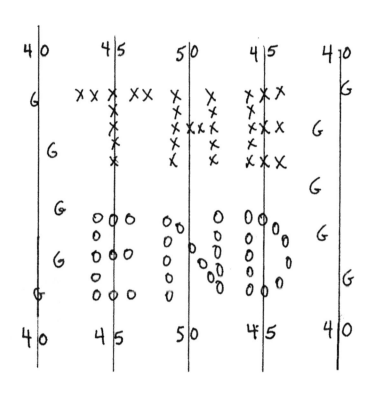

CREDITS

First, I'd like to thank everyone for their overwhelming support, especially my husband Jarrett. Without him, I couldn't have gotten this project done. Thanks to my parents for putting up with years and years of marching bands and bassoon lessons. I'd like to also thank all of the past and present TFBC readers for their support and contributions. Band nerds unite!!

A big thanks goes out to all of the band directors I've ever had as teachers. A little bit of each of them is in each comic: Patricia Jameson, Larry McLure, John Culvahouse, Dwight Satterwhite, and Darryl Jachens.

The *Tales From Band Camp* title font is *Creepy*, and the font used in the speech balloons is *WildandCrazy*. *SF Slapstick Comic* is used for the captions in the Band Nerd section.

You can read more TFBC comics at: http://www.talesfrombandcamp.com

Thanks to the following TFBC readers for their "You Know You're a Band Nerd When…" contributions:

Amelia from Bloomington, IN *
Benjamin from Sparta, TN *
Jennifer from Anaheim, CA*
Katie from Wyoming, MI*
Sherri from Austin, TX*
Rachel from Montgomery, AL*
Mary from Richfield, OH*
Jeanie from Brecksville, OH*
Chrissy from Eldersburg, MD*
Lara from Kenosha, WI*
Joey from El Cajon, CA*
Brandi from Canton, OH*
Kerami from Eagle Lake, FL*
Travis from Washington, PA*
Ruth from Baltimore, MD*
Lauren from Pawley's Island, SC*
Mary from Newbrighton, MN*

Laura from The Woodlands, TX
Katie from MCHS
Kristin from Vacaville, CA*
Denise from Philadelphia, PA*
Derrick from Alleman*
Adri from Austin, TX*
Shawna from Palm Desert, CA*
Karen from Tulsa, OK*
Shanna from Anderson, SC*
Mandie from Vancouver, WA*
Kensie from Enola, PA*
Alison from Philippi, WV
Pedro from Miami Springs, FL*
Ally from Pelion, SC*
Leslye from Walterboro, SC*
SOLSEN98 from Villa Park, CA*
Chris from Atlanta, GA

* couldn't confirm name

Printed in the United States
74967LV00003B/29